Old Devon Recip[es]

by

Catherine Rothwell

C000057767

Published by Richard Netherwood Ltd, Fulstone Barn, New Mill, Huddersfield, West Yorkshire
Text © Catherine Rothwell 1991
Printed in Yugoslavia by Gorenjski Tisk P.O.

Chudleigh Market Town was almost completely destroyed by fire in 1897. Fortunately the ancient building which housed Devon schoolboys from 1668 still stands. This grammar school was founded by John Pynsent. It is said that another John - Dryden - completed his succesful translation of Vergil at Chudleigh Rocks. This early 1900's photograph of Fore Street shows premises on the right claiming 'established since the time of Milton'.

Fore Street Chudleigh.

Introduction

"I often wish that I had clear
For life, 600 pounds a year,
A handsome house to lodge a friend,
A river at my garden's end..."

Whenever we come to Devon, beautiful county of fulfilled promise and pleasant surprise, setting aside that now absurd figure of 600, Jonathan Swift's sentiments in 1727 are mine today. Abounding in brimming rivers, there are many such desirable places as the Dean longed for; indeed we stayed at one the last night of our 1989 visit:20 acres shooting; high-walled garden; ice house; terrace; pheasants strutting in the long driveway and thick woods, at the end of which raced the River Mole. In the 18th Century it had all belonged to a rich woollen merchant, with a mill at his garden's end, a man so prosperous he could commission Adam work and have executed true Devon, Ipplepen marble columns for his handsome house.

Devonshire is dear to the hearts of many, each having his or her own idea of the county's essence in a nutshell. Sir Walter Raleigh rated it "the county of red earth, ruddy apples, rosy cheeks and honest men". Equally appreciative, lesser mortals have thought of a land of cream and roses, colour-washed houses, purple buddleia and of pink hydrangeas, but all would surely agree on its variety. Unique in English counties, having two coastlines, a close second in size to Yorkshire, its rich diversity grew on us day by day as we journeyed: wide expanses of moorland with thickly-wooded combes furrowing to the ocean; village clusters of thatched cottages with a wealth of 14th and 15th century churches; ancient buildings; manor houses; parks; farms; tumuli; cliffs; sandy and shingly beaches; inlets where myrtles and geraniums still bloomed. We were savouring Devon in the quiet of early autumn, a discovery in itself. Although we remember long-stay holidays when our children were young, uninterrupted by motor cars, we now revelled in winding miles of high-hedged lanes washed clean and sparkling by the rains of the previous night.

We were in search of recipes inseparable from history and tradition. As one hotel proprietor said, "You have come to the right place". Devonians, after a seemingly endless season, had time to talk. A circle of Armada cannons in the open air at Bideford made history seem tangible. Barnstaple furnished five ships which joined Sir Francis Drake's fleet at Plymouth to defeat the Spanish, all sailing from the Great Quay in 1588. With such an abundance of coaching inns: the Cherub at Dartmouth; the 14th century Rising Sun at Lynmouth or the Mill Inn, "last pub for miles", it was easy to conjure up scenes from 200 years ago, when bowls of hot punch or mulled wine, with handy ladles, were set in readiness for the coachmen who, although provided with a bear or tiger skin to throw over their knees, arrived in winter almost frozen stiff.

"Shark wreck and mackerel fishing" at Lynmouth, as a notice, may have been unique. The feat of its lifeboatmen between Thursday and Friday of January 12th-13th 1899 surely was. This rescue of the crew of the Forrest Hall crippled off Porlock involved 18 horses hauling lifeboat Louisa 11 up Countisbury Hill and over Exmoor. Launching at Lynmouth not being possible, they made for Porlock Weir, en route having to demolish a cottager's wall and at Ashton Gate put the lifeboat on skids. Ten and a half hours later on Friday the 13th at 6.30 a.m. the Louisa was launched, reaching the wreck one hour later. Supermen! But this astounding story was followed by another two days later on our tour. Not all that long ago, Devon men feared to work outside without a dog to keep off the pixies.

The isolation of the Moor, for no true Devonian calls it Dartmoor, is awe-inspiring. Still a weird and dangerous place for the unwary, no wheeled vehicles could penetrate a century ago. Only travellers and pack horses made their way along the tracks between bogs marked by granite crosses and relics from man's earliest civilizations. Westman's Wood is a remnant of ancient oak forest, 1,000 years old. On the moor, Stannary Law prevailed, the tin miners or stanners of Ashburton, Chagford, Plympton and Tavistock holding their own parliament in the open air at Crockern Tor. I delighted in villages where time is measured by the seasons, whose quaint names(some of which appear on no maps) include Martinhoe, Woody Bay, Kittitoe, Beccott, Snapper, but I missed the more dainty, rich-red cows of my childhood days, all of which seem to have been substituted by hulking black and white cattle. Sadly, we never saw a badger trundling along by the roadside, only dead ones knocked down by cars. To see the real Devon you have to leave your car and trudge over Exmoor or along the lanes between the 10 ft. high hedges, some 8 ft. across, alive with many species of bird, insect, plant and mammal.

To discover the real Devonian you have to talk about food. Response was as rich and varied as the coloured county itself. Many types and ages were generous, imparting the information we sought. We had indeed come to the right place.

Catherine Rothwell

Fishing boat 'Lucy' is high and dry at a Devon quay, whilst the tide has ebbed. The on-going task of drying and mending nets is evidenced by the hanging nets in the background, used for seine fishing. This 1890 photograph was taken when Brixham was a great fishing port with trawlers so successful they became models for huge fleets at ports which rose later at Fleetwood and Hull.

Eve Martin, National Trust Manageress at Arlington Court, served a variety of good soups: fresh vegetable; leek and potato; spicy orange and tomato, but reported that although the Sunday roast was still popular, almost 50% of her customers now favoured vegetarian dishes, such as leeks in a cream
cheese sauce with plenty of ground hazelnuts and almonds as topping.

Rules from the Servants' Hall of such great houses as Arlington Court, make amusing reading: " If any one be observed wiping their knives in the table cloth at any time, forfeit three pence. If any person use any indecent langauge when the cloth is on the table he is to forfeit three pence. All stable and other persons to come to dinner with their coats on."

I was interested to hear that at Arlington Court **Snow Pancakes** were made as in the higher parts of Lancashire:

3 tablespoons flour	1 egg
3 tablespoons snow	1/2 pint milk fresh from the
lard for frying	cow

Mix flour with milk by degrees and with the egg well beaten. Just before frying, put in the snow. Beat up quickly and add to the frying pan, sugaring and stacking each pancake in a warm place. The clean snow made them wonderfully light.

Devonshire Clotted Cream

"Nothing on earth, or in poet's dream
Is so rich or rare as Devonshire cream."

The traditional recipe for clotted cream being:
"In a wide bowl place your fresh, not pasteurised, milk. Leave it to stand. In summer the time would be 10 hours, in winter 24 hours. The bowl is then placed on low heat. Sometimes the slab of an old coal-fired range was a suitable temperature. It should be warmed very gradually to just below boiling point and this temperature maintained, but the milk should never actually boil. A thick crust was allowed to form on the top of the milk. Until the following day the bowl was stood in a cool place, after which the clotted ('clouted' in old Devon) cream was ready to be skimmed off."

One receipe I never attempted as I was sure it would not work for a "foreigner" unless the pixies lent a hand.

West Country Tart

6 oz shortcrust pastry	8 oz golden syrup
1 oz brown sugar, pounded	3 oz finely chopped walnuts
2 eggs	

Line a greased dish with shortcrust pastry. Beat together the eggs, the slightly warmed syrup, the sugar and the walnuts. Put this filling in the pastry case and bake in a moderate oven for 1/2 hour. When cold, it sets. This was traditionally served with cream. In testing I found that a scatter of shortbread mixture, just a flurry of the fine crumbs, on top of the fillings was an improvement, the mixture being less likely to brown round the edges. Definitely for the sweet toothed!

Treacle Tart from Simonsbath

"Line a shallow, buttered dish with shortcrust pastry. Put in about 3 tablespoons treacle, then scatter on 3 oz fine breadcrums. Finish off with lemon juice. Bake for 20 minutes in a hot oven."

Lard was used in making the shortcrust, 4 oz rubbed lightly into 8 oz flour until finely crumbled, when it was bound with a little iced water.

Meat Pasty

1 lb shortcrust pastry	6 oz potatoes
12 oz raw mutton or steak	1 small onion
seasoning	3 tablespoons cold water

Make the pastry and roll out to about 1/4 inch thick. Cut into rounds, using a saucer or small plate. Cut up the meat into small pieces, rejecting anything inedible such as gristle, lumps of fat or bone. Dice the raw potato and finely chop the onion. Mix the meat, onion and potato together very thoroughly, add salt and pepper and about 3 tablespoons of cold water. Place some of this filling on one half of each circle of pastry, damp the edges of the latter with cold water and fold over to cover the mixture. Press the edges of the pastry together and crimp it with the fingers to seal. Make two or three ventilating slits in the "lid", brush with beaten egg or milk if a glaze is required and place on a baking tray. Cook in a hot oven 200 C. until the pastry is pale brown, then reduce the heat to 180 C. for about 40 minutes.

Mary Hobbs of Clovelly still makes traditional herb pasties, and young Michelle Luke, also of Clovelly, told us of her grandmother's Taty Pasties, the filling of which consists of sliced potatoes and cream.

Herb Pasty

Chop a quantity of well washed parsley, watercress or spinach. Cut up finely some shallots or leeks and one or two rashers of bacon. Place the vegetables and bacon on rounds of shortcrust pastry (as for Meat Pasty), crimp each pasty except at one point, and pour into this a small amount of beaten egg. Seal the pasties and bake as usual.

Meat or Herb Pasties would be excellent fare for a train journey and hotels like Lyndale and Tors Park, both at Lynmouth, used to put up picnic hampers for visitors.

The 1895 Ward Lock and Bowden's Guide to Torquay and Dartmouth advertiser the Lynton, Lynmouth and Barnstaple fast four-horse coach 'Tanvity'. "...carrying the mails, it runs daily through the year (Sundays excepted)". Additional coaches during the summer season were 'Glen Lyn' and 'Tally Ho', all Messrs. Jones Bros.' fast four-horse coaches. The 3.21 train from Barnstaple Junction brought passengers to Waterloo, London in 7 hours once the 'Tantivy' had deposited them at the railway station.

The Tors Park Hotel, under Cecil H. Bevan, advertised 20 miles of trout and salmon fishing, 2,000 acres of shooting and the only tennis court in Lynmouth. The Devon and Somerset Foxhounds met 'within easy distance of the hotel'.

On the River Dart, naval vessels, pleasure yachts, trawlers and ferries are to be seen, the last-mentioned crossing between Dartmouth and Kingswear. There have been many historic sailings from here, the Crusades in 1147 and an American fleet in 1944 which left on D.Day. This photograph of Dartmouth's unspoiled river front was taken in 1924.

Warfleet, Dartmouth

5187

Early Summer Hotch Potch

1 quart good mutton stock	4 young carrots
6 Spring onions	1 small cauliflower
2 young turnips	1 sprig each of fresh parsley
1 cup freshly shelled peas	and thyme
1 lettuce (cabbage shaped)	

The young vegetables should be washed, carrots and turnips cut small, lettuce pulled apart leaf by leaf and the shallot onions chopped well, including the greentops. Put all, with parsley and thyme, into the good mutton stock and simmer for 1/2 hour. Then add the peas and the washed white part of the cauliflower, broken into small, dainty sprigs. Simmer on until these also are cooked. The whole process takes about one hour. Season towards the end. The old way was also to put left-over meat from the joint, a few minutes before serving, into the hotch potch, but it is not now considered advisable to warm meat in this way. The young vegetables are a wonderful treat in themselves.

We ate a simple but excellent soup at The Spinney, Shirwell, prepared by Janet Pelling, based on rich bone stock with an assortment of autumn vegetables. A scattering of fresh parsley on each portion added more subtle flavour.

Laver

Laver, which used to be made at Watchet and Blue Anchor Bay, now seems to be confined to Barnstaple, where we found it selling briskly in Eric Hayes' shop. Eric advised that it be used freshly and explained: Gather the flat, green, filmy, ribbon-like laver (seaweed) preferably from rocks. Wash it well. Place it in a saucepan with vinegar and butter. Boil until it thickens. Put in jars. At one time the pickle was sealed with mutton fat. He recommended eating it with Hog's Pudding and sausages. Max Tey had told us that laver, gathered from sand is difficult to cleanse.

Standing by was trawlerman's son Peter Taylor who catches all kinds of fish in the Bay except halibut. He has caught eels up to 100 lb weight and reminded us of another traditional Barnstaple meal.

Salcombe, with one of the finest harbours in the West Country, is still a favourite haven of yatchtsmen. Its first regatta was held in 1857. This card dates from 1905 and shows the marine Hotel, then famous for its lobsters and seafood.

Marine Hotel, Salcombe

Saltwater Eels

Discard tail and bottom half. Cleanse, cut in pieces and simmer. Skin, then bake in a dish with bay leaves and spices, using 50% water, 50% vinegar.

Trawler owner Mr. S.R.A. Taylor said that the herring which disappeared for 25 years are now coming back. The Taylors' specialities are lobster, crab, taw salmon and sea trout. Chunks of haddock and prawns in rich cream made what was called Seafarers' Pie.

Marinated Herrings or Pilchards

Clean and fillet the fish then roll them up and put into a porcelain dish. Add 3 bay leaves and 2 teaspoons of pickling spice, a little pepper and salt, then cover and bake slowly at 300 F., 150 C., gas mark 2, for 2 1/2 hours. Some Devon housewives put a bay leaf into each rolled-up fish. The fish were left to go cold in the marinade.

Red Gurnard with Sauce

1 tablespoon wholemeal flour	1 tablespoon butter
1/2 pint good fresh stock	lemon juice
2 egg yolks	seasoning
1 red gurnard	

Cook the flour in the melted butter, stirring well. After 3 minutes add fish stock, stirring all the time. Remove from heat, stir in the strained egg yolks and lemon juice. Season to taste and pour all over the fish.

The fish is skinned and boned and poached gently in vinegar and water for 25 minutes after which it should be drained and flaked.

Shaldon Apple Pie and Cream

1 lb cooking apples	4 oz caster sugar
grated rind of 1/2 lemon	1 oz butter
pinch of cinnamon	1/2 lb shortcrust pastry

Butter a deep, enamelled plate and line it with the shortcrust pastry. Mix together the cinnamon, sugar and grated lemon rind. Peel, core and slice the apples, arranging the slices in layers. Sprinkle the cinnamon etc. between the layers. Pour over the melted butter. Cover with a pastry lid, pinching edges round the plate together to seal. Make a slit in the top and bake for 3/4 hour in a fairly hot oven. Traditionally served all over Devon with clotted cream.

At Marldon, Devon, the Apple Pie Fair takes place at the begining of August. Founded in 1888, it lapsed during the last war but was revived in 1958. Under a huge pie crust large quantities of little apples are baked. The pie is dragged to the fairground by a donkey, where portions are sold. The ceremony originated from the days when poor labourers relied on windfalls of apples to supplement their families' diet. Marldon decided long ago to bake one big pie in the communal bakehouse and have a village party.

Cockington village and forge, near Torquay, is a picturesque postcard settlement of thatched dwellings, dating from the Middle Ages. Sketched and photographed times without number, in the year of this photograph, 1928, it was described as 'one of the gems of Devon'.

COCKINGTON VILLAGE AND FORGE, TORQUAY.

Gooseberry and Elderflower Cream

1 lb gooseberries	4 oz fine sugar
4 heads elderflowers	1/4 pint double Devonshire cream

Rinse the gooseberries well, but there is no need to top and tail. Cook the gooseberries with the sugar over low heat for about 7 minutes. Add the elderflowers, washed. Stir well, leave for 5 minutes then take out the 4 heads of flowers. Sieve the fruit into a bowl and leave until cold, when you can fold in the stiffly whipped cream (do not over-whip it). Leave covered on a cold, marble slab until ready to dish up.

   Brannoc, a 16th. century Devon saint, taught the people of Brauton to till the soil and rear cattle. It was said he used wild deer to pull the plough. When someone stole his cow and put it in the cooking pot, St. Brannoc called it forth. Whole again, it continued to supply him with milk for a long time after this event.

Devon Roast Lamb

shoulder of lamb	3 small onions sliced
1 lb potatoes	seasoning
1 pint lamb stock	1 teaspoon chopped rosemary

Peel and slice the potatoes. Into a roasting tin put the sliced potatoes and onions. Put in the stock. Place the lamb on top, scattering with seasoning and the rosemary and put into a hot oven. Cook for 2 hours, lowering oven temperature towards the end of cooking, by which time some evaporation has allowed the potato tops to brown and the meat juices to flavour the vegetables. It is best to trim off any surplus fat from the joint before cooking.

Kingsteignton has a Ram Roasting Fair on the Spring Bank Holiday Monday based on a happening centuries ago. The stream that flowed through the churchyard and village suddenly dried up, only to reappear when a ram was sacrificed, so the custom continues.

Tavistock Beef with Dumplings
- the Beef

2 lb stewing beef cubed, all fat removed	1 cup cream
1 large Spanish onion, chopped	1 teaspoon black pepper
	1 teaspoon salt
2 pints home-made beef stock	3 oz butter
4 tablespoons flour	2 tablespoons cider
	1 bay leaf

Mix the flour, salt and pepper together and roll the beef cubes in the flour mixture. Heat the butter and brown the onion and beef cubes in it. Remove with a slatted spoon, placing meat and onions in a large, oven-proof casserole. Then pour in the cider, beef stock, bay leaf. Cover casserole and cook in a moderate oven for 2 hours.

- the Dumplings

2 beaten free-range eggs	8 oz breadcrumbs
4 tablespoons water	seasoning
2 tablespoons chopped, fresh parsley	1 grated onion

Put all in a mixing bowl, but add the water carefully. The dumpling mixture should not be soggy. Shape into small balls on a floured board and put in casserole 30 minutes before cooking time ends. Finally spoon over the cream just before serving. It looks mouth-watering brought to the table with a large ladle and lots of fresh crusty bread.

Good Wife Soup

1 quart good meat stock	2 medium-sized potatoes
2 oz butter	1 large leek
pinch of nutmeg	1 large Spanish onion
salt and pepper	

Clean the leek well, removing outer leaves, and chop well. Peel and slice onion very thinly. Clean, peel and dice the potatoes. Melt butter in a pan and fry the cut-up vegetables in it, gently for 5 minutes.
Add the stock and nutmeg. Season and simmer for half an hour. Serve with toast sippets.

Spinach Soup

2 lb freshly picked, washed spinach	freshly ground black pepper and sea salt
1/2 cup thin cream or top of milk	1/2 teacup water
	knob of butter

Cook spinach in water for 8 minutes. Puree in a liquidiser or push through a hair sieve in the old-fashioned way. Reheat, slowly adding butter, pepper, salt and milk, stirring all the time to ensure a smooth consistency. This is excellent before starting on the roast chicken.

Sheep's Head Soup

1 sheep's head	3 pints water
bunch of fresh herbs	1 carrot, 1 turnip, 1 large
1 small piece celery	Spanish onion
a few stalks of parsley	1 oz butter
1 tablespoon fine oatmeal	2 teaspoons pre-soaked barley
1 teaspoon tarragon vinegar	seasoning

The head should be washed very well and left to soak in warm, boiled water for an hour. Remove brains and tongue. Put the head in a large pan with the bunch of herbs, the vegetables all cleaned and chopped, a teaspoon of coarse salt and a sprinkling of black pepper. Add 3 pints of water and bring to the boil. Skim and simmer steadily with the fine oatmeal for 2 hours. Meanwhile, wash the brains, removing any fibre, and boil gently in slightly salted water for 15 minutes. Pound them, mixing with butter and a few breadcrumbs. Stir this into the soup and simmer on for 1 1/2 hours. Removing the meat from the head and put back into the soup, which will now be ready to serve. The tongue can be cooked along with the head, then skinned, to be used as a separate dish.

Fish Stock

Many fish soups were common in old Devon and the basis was a good fish stock made as follows:

2 lb raw fish bones and trimming	1/2 teaspoon coarse salt
6 white peppercorns	2 pints water
1 large Spanish onion	1/2 blade mace
1 large tomato	1 bay leaf and 1 sprig parsley
	1 small carrot

The basis was a hoch potch too - even shrimps shells and lobster shells going in, but mackerel and salmon were not used because these are too oily. All the trimmings were washed well and cut small, the herbs, spices were tied with a piece of muslin and the vegetables chopped small after washing.

Put all ingredients into stew pan, bring to the boil and skim. Then simmer slowly for 3/4 hour. Strain. Fish stock needs to be made freshly and used there and then.

Vegetable Marrow Soup

2 lb vegetable marrow, without seeds and peel	1 quart chicken stock
1 celery heart	1 onion
1/2 pint milk	bunch of herbs
1 teaspoon chopped chives	1 oz butter
1 slice of toast	2 oz dripping
	seasoning

Cut the vegetable marrow into cubes and place in stew pan with the chicken stock (preferably made by boiling chicken carcase), herbs, chopped celery heart, finely chopped onion. Boil gently for 2 minutes. Take out bunch of herbs and rub the soup through a sieve or liquidise. Return to stew pan, add milk and butter. Now adjust the seasoning with salt and black peppercorns, ground. Bring to the boil, sprinkle with the chives and serve with the diced toast fried crisply in the dripping. Old-fashioned sippets were made this way, beef or bacon dripping giving a good, meaty flavour. Cooked on low temperature, it takes 1/2 hour.

This 1895 photograph of Paignton was taken at a time when many improvements were afoot. A very old town, belonging to the see of Exeter before the Norman Conquest, it was also famous as a place where cider was manufactured on a large scale. In Springtime visitors came for miles to see the apples blossom.

Baked Brown Trout

Butter a fireproof dish, put in the washed trout, sprinkle with lemon juice and bake in a moderate oven for 20 minutes. The flavour of fresh, river trout is so good that like salmon it needs no other flavouring or sauce.

Baked Teign Trout

4 small trout	1 tablespoon white vinegar
1 shallot	sprig of thyme
1 teaspoon flour	1 teaspoon lemon juice
seasoning	

Clean trout and remove scales. Put the vinegar, thyme, chopped shallot and 3 tablespoons water into a pan with seasoning and simmer for 5 minutes. Strain this liquid into an oven-proof baking dish and put in the trout. Whilst cooking, baste well with the liquid over a period of 1/2 hour. Place the trout onto a hot dish. Sprinkle the teaspoon of flour into the liquor, add butter and stir until it boils. Keep stirring for 5 minutes more, so that the flour cooks. Add the lemon juice. Pour over the fish and serve.

"Trout tastes so wonderful because it feeds in the pure waters of streams flowing from Exmoor" - this from a couple with 20 acres and fishing rights along a stretch of the River Mole.

Oyster Soup

1 dozen fresh oysters	1 quart fish stock
1 teaspoon anchovy essence	1 teaspoon lemon juice
1 oz butter	1 dessertspoon flour

Place the oysters with their juices in a saucepan and place over gentle heat. Before they actually boil take off the fire, strain liquor and reserve it. The 'beards' of the oyster, i.e. the dark fringe round the edges, should be carefully cut off. Put the stock into a stewpan, add the 'beards' and oyster liquor and simmer for 20 minutes, then strain through a fine sieve and put the liquor back into the stewpan.

In the small pan melt the butter and sprinkle in the flour, stir while it cooks gently for a few minutes. Add gradually a teacup of stock, stir until very smooth then add to rest of stock. Put in the anchovy essence (100 years ago, pounded anchovy), bring to boil, stir all the time and boil for 5 minutes, putting in towards the end a light dusting of freshly ground pepper and the lemon juice.

Meanwhile, the quartered oysters are laid in a large soup tureen. The soup is poured over them and all is ready to serve. The traditional way with oysters is to eat them raw with a squeeze of lemon juice, brown bread and butter and a glass of white wine.

This photograph, almost a hundred years old, is of the natural arch 'London Bridge' which was made by the waves' surge over hundreds of years. Not far away was Meadfoot beach where in those days of segregation 'a thousand men might bathe simultaneously, for it is one of the finest beaches in the world'.

Devon Broth

1 quart mutton stock	1 cabbage heart
1 onion	1 carrot
1 turnip	1 leek
2 oz butter	3 oz pearl barley
a faggot of sweet herbs	a few sprigs of parsley
seasoning	

Peel onion and turnip, scrape carrot and wash the leek well by splitting open and running cold water through it. Shred the cabbage (separated leaf by leaf and well washed) and the leek. Chop finely the other vegetables including the parsley. Put the butter in a pan and quickly fry all the vegetables in it. Add the stock and simmer gently with the herbs and pearl barley which should have soaked overnight. After adjusting seasoning, take out herbs and serve the soup very hot. Another lady referred to the basic vegetable soup as Wintry Nights Soup. All these Devon soups are made superb by the quality of the stock and the freshness of vegetables.

A photograph taken on board a battleship in Plymouth or Portsmouth harbour in the 1920's. Captain James Cook, Charles Darwin, and the Pilgrim Fathers who sailed to America are all part of this famous town's history. Amongst this group are four cooks. In the days of the masted sailing ships 'loblolly' or sailors' gruel, was a dish served to crews when rations were low.

Torbay Mussels

Mussels were once found in large quantities. The shells should be tightly closed. If mussels float in water they are not fresh. The shells should be well washed and scrubbed then soaked in salted water. Finally rinse under a running tap in a colander. Place the mussels wet into a strong, iron pan. Cover and place over a moderate fire. Keep shaking the pan. As soon as the mussels open they are ready. Strain off the liquor and keep for making fish stock. Turn the mussels out, beard them and serve on a white, damask napkin (the beard can be removed with scissors).

Mussels made into sauce for baked flounder and fresh grey sole or megrim and haddock were once popular in Devon, but the megrim had to be used as fresh as possible or it soon loses all flavour.

Sole in Cider

4 fillets of sole	1/2 pint of cider
1 oz butter mixed with	seasoning
1 teaspoon flour	chives

Place the fillets into an oven-proof dish. Pour the cider over them and bake at 180 C., 350 F., gas mark 4, for 30 minutes. Strain the liquid into a saucepan and put in the worked-together flour and butter. Cook for five minutes until it thickens. Float in some snipped chives and pour over the fillets of sole which have meanwhile been kept warm. Torbay sole is noted for quality and sometimes referred to as witch sole.

Turbot in Cider

4 turbot steaks	1/2 pint Devon cider
squeeze of lemon	2 oz butter
1 teaspoon chopped chives	seasoning

Wash the turbot steaks and pat dry. Place in an oven-proof dish spread with the mixed butter and chives, then add cider, lemon juice and seasoning. Cover and bake in a moderate oven for 25 minutes, basting half way through and at the end.

Jugged Hare with Redcurrant Jelly

Traditionally served the day after Christmas Day, the hare left marinating in the cold pantry for 2 days prior to cooking.

This view is of Barnstaple's Bouthport Street in 1919. 'The Horse and Groom' inn shown on the right, we noticed as we walked past in October 1989, is now much enlarged. Another old inn is the 'Three Tuns'. In 1850 there were 26 beerhouses and 56 inns and taverns. Barnstaple also had at that time 16 maltsters and 23 grocers and tea dealers. Names which featured then are still around today: Bowden; Quick; Soper; Thorne. Said to be the oldest Borough in England, is still has the Tome Stone, resembling a sun dial, on Georgian Queen Anne's Walk, where merchants and shipowners struck bargains.

- the marinade

1 glass tarragon vinegar	1 glass Dev
1 onion sliced	4 crushed
3 bay leaves	salt and
2 oz butter	

Melt the butter and mix all in to form the marinade; the on be very thinly sliced. The washed, jointed hare was placed in marinade and turned several times during the 2 days.

Having removed the hare joints from the marinade, pat dry and gently brown in butter. Place them in a deep, oven-proof dish with a layer of finely chopped vegetables at the bottom (celery, carrot, onion, parsley) just enough to cover the dish. Scatter more chopped parsley and fresh thyme mixed with 1 tablespoon of flour over the joints. Add water until it comes 3/4 way up the pot. Cover tightly and cook in a moderate oven for 3 hours. Half an hour before cooking time is up, stir in 3 tablespoons of redcurrant jelly.

Some like to thicken the hare gravy with cornflour, but my father, who took his cooking seriously, never did this. He served jugged hare with freshly picked, hot red cabbage.

Pheasant with Apple Sauce

1 large pheasant (it should be hung for 3 days)
2 tablespoons butter

other wrapped the breast of the prepared bird with rashers
bacon and placed it with the butter in the roasting tin.
ne the weight, allowing 20 minutes to the lb and 15 minutes
ooking in a moderate oven. The bird was covered with folded,
pened greaseproof paper as well, which was lifted for basting
rposes during cooking, then replaced, but removed entirely 15
ninutes before the end.

For the apple sauce you need:

1 lb Devon apples	1/4 pint cider
1 oz butter	pinch of cinnamon

Melt the butter and place in the peeled, cored, sliced apples. Stew
very gently indeed. The apples should not fall, the secret being to
slice them very thinly; thus they will keep their shape. Add a pinch
of cinnamon and finally the cider. Simmer on over low heat until
the sauce thickens. Serve hot with the roast pheasant.

Hancock's Devon Cider, one of four local ciders, is made at
Clapworthy Mill, North Devon. Winners of over 40 prizes for real
cider, all are produced by traditional methods.

Devonshire Brawn

I am told that rabbit brawn was also traditional in Devon but the
boar, and later its descendant the pig, especially at Christmas time
seem to have been the norm.

1 pig's cheek	1 pig's ear
3 large trotters	1 tongue
seasoning	pinch of powdered mace

All the meat must be thoroughly scalded and put into a stew pot.
Cover with cold water and bring to the boil. After skimming, simmer
on for 2 hours until the meat is falling from the bones. Remove the
bones and cut the meat up, removing any fat and allowing to go
cold. The meat is now jellied and should be put back into the stew
pot. Put on gentle heat; season with salt, pepper and mace. Simmer
on for 10 minutes then turn into a mould and leave to set. Do not
cut into it until quite cold.

Devonshire rabbit or pig's brawn was always accompanied with
mustard, the brawn cut into thick slices, the English mustard mixed
with cream.

*The 16th century smugglers' cottages at Lee Bay by the early 20th
century had become 'Devon Pottery, Gifts, Souvenirs, Curios'. Notices
on the left also advertise light lunches which consisted of Devonshire
pasties, soup and ices.*

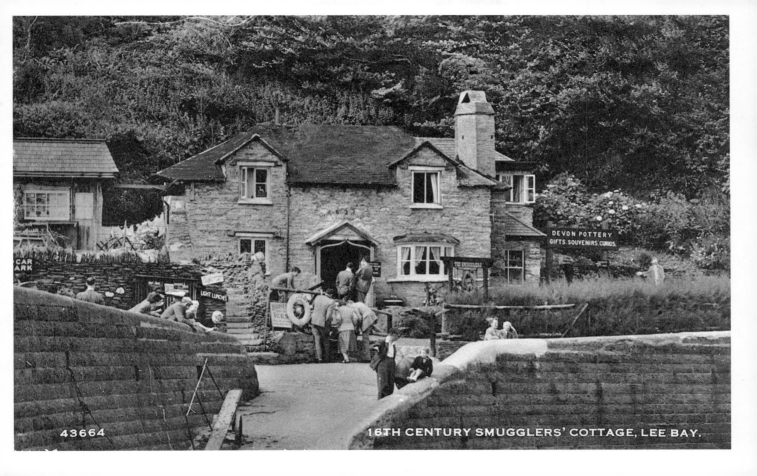

43664   16TH CENTURY SMUGGLERS' COTTAGE, LEE BAY.

Exeter Stew

2 lb cubed shoulder steak rolled in seasoned flour
2 large Spanish onions sliced thinly
1 pint good beef stock
3 stalks washed celery or chopped celery heart

1/2 teaspoon marjoram
some beef dripping
1/2 lb parsnips cut up
1/2 pint Devon cider
seasoning

The sliced onions are cooked in the beef dripping, then with the stock and cider are put with the cubed, floured meat. Let it simmer for a while then put in the majoram and chopped vegetables. Season well and simmer gently for 2 hours by which time the meat should be tender.

This stew was accompanied by dumplings which were put into the pot 1/2 hour before the stew was ready, enough time to cook them and imbue with a beefy flavour.

These were made as follows:

4 oz flour
a good pinch of mixed herbs
water

2 oz shredded suet
seasoning

Mix the dry ingredients and bind with a little water. Do not make the dough sticky. Roll into 6 small balls and drop them into the Exeter Stew. At North Molton these were referred to as 'pretty dumplings'.

Leeky Frizzle

8 lambs chops
seasoning
1 lb cleaned, chopped leeks

2 lb mashed potatoes
1 teaspoon rosemary

The potatoes should be cooked and mashed with thin cream and butter. Spread this mash on the base and sides of a big, glazed, terra-cotta dish. Chop the leeks well and lay over the potato. Place the chops on top of all, well sprinkled with rosemary, and roast in a really hot oven until browned and crisp. It takes about an hour.

Summer Herb Tart

6 oz plain flour
1 egg yolk twirled into
1 tablespoon milk
2 eggs yolks
seasoning
2 oz butter

2 eggs
2 oz mixed fresh parsley and chives well chopped
3/4 pint single Devonshire cream

Sieve the flour and rub in the butter, using a deep baking bowl. Mix to dough with the egg yolk and milk. Roll out to fit a shallow tart tin, gently pricking the base of the pastry. Bake in a moderate oven 200 C., 400 F., gas mark 6, for only 15 minutes. Beat the eggs and egg yolks with the cream. Stir in the herbs and seasoning. Pour carefully and slowly into the cooked pastry case and place the tart tin on a baking sheet. Bake until the filling is set and serve it hot. It's much nicer that way.

Oddicombe Beach, a fine sandy beach at the foot of Babbacombe Downs, in 1900 was completely secluded from the busy world. It was one of the three beaches in the area where mixed bathing was allowed. A tiny Refreshment Hut can be seen dwarfed by high cliffs from where strawberries and cream, jugs of tea and thickly buttered scones could be bought.

Our last trip into Devon was at harvest time. Markets everywhere had splendid displays of fruit and vegetables, amongst the latter, healthy-looking kale, cauliflowers, kohl rabi, cabbage and broccoli plus a great selection of fresh herbs, honey and cheeses. Thoughts and conversation turned to the harvest suppers of a century and more ago "When cut and come again was the order of the evening". Passed down memories from by-standing Devonions: "Buckets of taties mashed with lard and cabbage"; "Beer, cider and frothing horns of ale", but first the celebrating harvesters lifted the neck of corn dressed with gay ribbons and set it on the mantlepiece. Bacon and peas were cooked with a saddle of mutton and sausages. "Plum pudding was placed on pewter plates with the mutton". Harvest songs were then sung and much raising of pots and tankards as farmers and villagers roared: "The corn, oh, the corn, 'tis the rippening of the corn ..." Mincemeat in those days was made from golden pippin apples finely shredded, with spices, vine friuts and finely shredded undercut of sirloin of beef.

Devon Saddle of Lamb with Redcurrant Jelly

A saddle of lamb featured often on the bills of fare at the old coaching inns which served up the choicest of food. Far too large for today's families, it is still interesting to know how "a saddle" was dealt with. A saddle consists of the 2 loins together from rib to tail. The kidneys were cooked separately of course.

Cover the saddle with chopped rosemary and dust with pepper, pouring on a small quantity of melted dripping and place in a large roasting tin. The oven should be pre-heated to 200 C., 400 F., gas mark 4, and the meat cooked at 20 minutes to the lb. thus a 12 lb. saddle would take 4 hours and it was necessary to keep the meat well basted all the time.

The redcurrant jelly was made as follows:

Cover 3 lb redcurrants with water and simmer for 30 minutes. Strain or leave to drip overnight through a flannel jelly bag. Next day, allowing 1lb sugar to every pint of juice, simmer till sugar has dissolved then boil quickly for 15 minutes to achieve a set. Pour into clean, warmed jars.

Rabbit with Cream

1 rabbit	2 oz butter
1 chopped celery heart	1 medium chopped onion
1/2 pint cider	1/4 pint cream
bunch of herbs	seasoned flour

Wipe and joint the rabbit, rolling the joints in the seasoned flour. Heat the butter and toss the chopped celery into it. Cook gently for 5 minutes. Place in a casserole, then brown the rabbit in the butter, with the onions. Put these also into the casserole, season, and pour in the cider, the bunch of herbs and the cream. Cook in a moderate oven until the rabbit is tender. It takes about 2 hours. In Devon small balls made of sage and onion stuffing with chopped bacon are sometimes served with the rabbit.

1818   LYNTON AND LYNMOUTH CLIFF RAILWAY

The Lynton and Lynmouth Cliff Railway was sponsored to link the two after the construction of the narrow gauge railway from Barnstaple to Lynton which operated from 1898-1935. The Cliff Railway is water powered as it makes its precipitous descent, the two carriages being counter-balanced by 700 gallon water tanks.

Salmon Tail in Cream

Brixham sent fish to London and Bath in the 18th. century and by the 19th. was the best-known fish market in Devon. London-bound fish were sent by sea, but inland it was carried by pack horses.

1 tail end of salmon
1/4 pint thick cream
cider

Butter an oven-proof dish. Put in the tail and season it well. Pour over the cider, sufficient to come half way up the sides of the dish and bake for 1/2 hour in a moderate oven. Take out the fish, skin it and remove the bones. The juices in which it was cooked should be rapidly boiled to reduce quantity. Pour this over the fish and finish off with the thick cream also poured. Another 10 minutes in the oven and the salmon is ready to serve.

Hog's Pudding

2 lb belly of pork, minced
1 tablespoon dried sage
salt and black pepper

8 oz fresh breadcrumbs
1/2 teaspoon thyme

Mix all ingredients together, making sure that the herbs are evenly distributed. Shape the meat into sausages with floured hands. Dust with more flour. Put to stand in a cold place and cook after 3 hours, either frying or if the mixture is to be baked, in small, greased tins. Do not overfill the tins. Place in a moderate oven for about 20 minutes. The pudding can also go into pasties with the addition of chopped onion and turnip.

Another Brawn Recipe

1/2 pig's head
1 teaspoon ground nutmeg
water and sprig of parsley

1 large Spanish onion
8 peppercorns
1 bay leaf

Scrub the 1/2 head well and put into a large saucepan with all the ingredients except the nutmeg. Cover with cold water and bring to the boil. Reduce to simmer and continue for 3 hours. Lift out the head and gather up all the meat which will be loose from the bone. Remove tongue and skin. Chop all the meats up as finely as possible. Boil up the liquid in which the 1/2 head was cooked and reduce it in quantity. Strain this and cool it. Add the nutmeg to the meat and give a generous pepper and salt addition. Place in a dish. Any fat should be lifted from the cooled, jellied stock and poured over the meat. Cover the dish and put in a cold place to set. Parsley is a good garnish to decorate the brawn when turned out of its dish and salad is quite the best accompaniment.

Dartmouth Pie

8 oz shortcrust pastry
4 boned chops of pork with fat removed
freshly ground pepper and salt
2 peeled, sliced onions

pinch of nutmeg
1 pint cider
4 large apples, cored, peeled and sliced

Put 2 of the chops in a deep pie dish then a layer of apples sprinkled with seasoning, sugar and spice. Next lay slices of onion. Repeat this, seasoning as you go. Pour in the cider. Make a fairly thick pastry crust to cover the pie dish. To allow steam to escape, make a hole in the top. Brush with egg yolk and milk whisked together and bake in a moderate oven for 1 1/4 hours. Some people add cream but this is rather too rich with pork.

Lantern Hill, Ilfracombe, was photographed in July 1923. "My dear Brighteye," reads this card, "....
glorious weather and there is plenty of good tucker." Devon's largest holiday resort developed in the 19th. century, but it had been a safe haven for fishing boats for a long time, Ilfracombe's sheltered harbour being at the foot of craggy Lantern Hill.

Lantern Hill, Ilfracombe

Appledore Parsnip Cakes

This recipe came from a country pub which served the cakes with Sunday roast.

1 lb parsnips	1 beaten egg
2 tablespoons flour	seasoning
1 breakfast cup breadcrumbs	1 oz butter

Peel and clean the parsnips, boiling in water until soft. Drain and mash them thoroughly. Add the flour, seasoning and butter. Mix well and form into flat, round cakes. Dip in beaten egg and scatter with the breadcrumbs. Fry on both sides until nicely browned. They are made in much the same way as Lancashire potato cakes.

Devonport Veal and Ham Pie

8 oz shortcrust pastry	1 lb veal
1 lb ham	2 hard-boiled eggs
seasoning	1 teaspoon marjoram
1 medium-sized, chopped onion	egg to glaze the pastry

Cook the veal with the marjoram and 1 chopped onion in water for an hour, then chop and mix with the ham. In a big, deep pie dish layer the meat with the 2 eggs in the centre, the seasoning and the rest of the onion. Using the stock in which the veal was cooked, pour this carefully into the pie dish until it is 3/4 full. Cover with pastry, brush with egg and make a small hole in the top of the crust to let out the steam. Bake at 220 C., 425 F., gas mark 7, for 20 minutes, then lower the heat. If served really cold, it will have a tasty veal jelly inside.

Torquay Fruit and Nut Gingerbread

This excellent ginger parkin was served as pudding, with custard, cream or yoghurt, but we found that it was splendid as cake. Any left over improves with keeping.

4 oz oats	4 oz plain flour
1 level teaspoon bicarb of soda	2 level teaspoons ground ginger
4 oz treacle	2 oz syrup
2 oz butter	1 oz brown sugar
milk to mix	3 oz sultanas
3 oz chopped Brazil nuts	

Grease and line a rectangular tin 9 ins. by 6 ins. Sieve flour, ginger, bicarbonate of soda. Add oats. Prepare by the melting method i.e. warm syrup and treacle with sugar and butter. Add milk to give a batter-like consistency. Mix all together very well, adding sultanas and chopped nuts. Bake at 150 C., 300 F., gas mark 3 for one hour. Allow to cool before you attempt to turn it out or it will break up.

Exmouth in the 16th. century was very important and used as a base by Sir Walter Raleigh. The clock tower shown was a gift to the town from the Lord of the Manor, Mark Rolle, on the occasion of Queen Victoria's Diamond Jubilee. A favourite 18th. century Georgian town, its mild air was recommended for invalids.

Esplanade and Beach, Exemouth

Valentine's Series

D P
June 2nd 05

Sidmouth Apple Pudding

1/2 lb apples	1 pint milk
1 breakfast cup breadcrumbs	1 egg
2 oz butter	2 oz caster sugar
a pinch of cinnamon	

Peel, core and chop the apples. Beat the egg and the sugar together. The milk is then heated with the breadcrumbs and cinnamon. As it heats up put in 1 oz butter. Take off the fire and when it has cooled, add the beaten egg and sugar and the apples. Butter a pie dish and bake in a moderate oven for an hour.

Woolacombe Apple Cake

1 lb cooking apples, sliced and peeled	2 tablespoons water
	2 whole cloves
4 oz brown sugar	4 oz butter
2 tablespoons floured, seedless raisins	2 eggs
	1 teaspoon baking powder
4 oz breadcrumbs	2 oz flour

Cook the apples until they 'fall', with the water, sugar and cloves. Sieve. Remove the cloves. Beat with the egg yolks and add the butter, melted, then the dried fruit. Whip the egg whites and fold in with the flour, breadcrumbs and baking powder. Mix well and put into a floured cake tin. Cook in a moderate oven for 3/4 hour.

Crediton Pan Cake

A cake made in a pan on top of the stove or 'slab'.

1/2 lb sultanas and currants	1/2 pint milk
1 egg	11 oz flour
4 oz butter	2 oz dripping or lard
pinch of salt	

Beat the milk and egg together and mix well. Mix the flour, salt, butter and lard well then add the egg and milk. Finally stir in the dried fruits. Roll out on a floured board, making it the size of the base of the pan bottom and put the cake upon it. Cook slowly so that the cake browns top and bottom. It can be more convienietly cooked in the oven on moderate heat for 1 hour. Then split open with a warmed, sharp carving knife and spread with butter.

Devon Cream Biscuits from Dawlish Warren

8 oz clotted cream	1 lb plain flour
4 oz caster sugar	1 large beaten egg
1 1/2 tablespoons milk	

Sift the flour into the clotted cream. Add the egg, working the mixture with the fingertips until it is like very fine crumbs. Add the sugar, setting aside 1 oz. Add a very little milk and roll out thinly this pastry-like mixture on a floured board. Cut into small rounds and sprinkle each with the remaining sugar. Place on a greased baking tray and bake at 200 C., 400 F., gas mark 6 for 15 minutes.

Teignmouth Honey Cake

8oz flour	6 oz butter
3 oz Devon honey	2 eggs

Sift the flour and pour the warmed honey and butter into the well of flour mix. Add the beaten eggs and beat all the mixtures well together. Bake in a buttered tin for one hour at 125 C., 250 F., gas mark 1.

At the Quince Honey Farm, South Molton, where we stoppped for Devon honey, wild colonies and unique observation hives behind glass can be watched in safety. It is acknowledged to be the world's best honeybee exhibition.

Exeter Old High Street shows one example of its ancient buildings, this one photographed in 1909. A plaque marks the spot where one timber-framed Tudor building stood, but which, because it was in the way of a new road, had to be jacked up and rolled to a new site. A display of the world-famous Honiton lace, which Queen Victoria and royal babies wore, is on show in Exeter's Musuem.

Ginger Snaps

1/2 lb flour	of soda dissolved in
1/4 lb brown sugar	1 tablespoon hot water
1/2 oz ground ginger	1/4 syrup
1 level saltspoon bicarbonate	a large nut of butter

Rub the butter into the flour, add the sugar and ginger, then mix in the syrup. The soda dissolved in hot water should be tipped in last and quickly. Roll out, cut into biscuits and bake in a moderate oven for 15 minutes.

Lamb Stew

3 lb boned lamb, cubed	2 medium onions, sliced
2 crushed garlic cloves	1/2 teaspoon salt
1 teaspoon ground cumin	1/2 teaspoon black pepper
4 tablespoons vegetable oil	1 1/2 cups dry sherry

In a large mixing bowl place the lamb, garlic and sherry. Combine well and leave to marinate for 4 hours.

Remove the lamb, pat dry and save the marinade. Sprinkle the lamb with salt, pepper and cumin. Place the oil in a large saucepan. Add the pieces of lamb and fry them for 5 minutes with the onions. Pour over the marinade and bring to the boil. Reduce to a simmer and with the pan covered, simmer the stew for 1 1/2 hours. Serve very hot with crusty bread rolls and watercress.

Devonshire Splits

1/2 lb plain flour	1 teaspoon salt
1/2 oz butter	1/2 oz yeast
1 teaspoon sugar	1/4 pint warm milk

Sieve flour and salt into a warm bowl. Rub in butter. Cream yeast and sugar, adding the warmed milk (not hot). Make a well in the flour. Add the yeast and liquid, beating well in to form a soft dough. Cover bowl and set in a warm place until the dough has doubled. On a floured board knead lightly then divide the dough into 6 pieces. Knead each into a round shape and place the splits on a floured baking tray until they have doubled in size (about 15 minutes). Brush tops with milk and bake in a hot oven for 20 minutes until brown and risen. They should sound hollow when tapped underneath. Cool on a wire tray. Splits are favoured for Devon teas, filled with home-made strawberry jam and clotted cream.

Roast Duck and Chestnuts

1 lb chestnuts	2 oz butter
1 pint hot water	seasoning
1 duck about 6 lb weight	1 chopped onion
sprigs of washed parsley	1 celery heart

The stuffing is made by cutting a slit in each chestnut and boiling in water for 15 minutes. Drain and peel. Melt the butter and sweat the chopped celery heart in it. Add the chestnuts, about 1/2 pint of the hot water, season and simmer on for 15 minutes, keeping the mixture well stirred.

The prepared duck should be wiped inside after washing and

stuffed with the chestnut and celery mixture. Prick the skin of the duck all over and place in a roasting tin. Roast at 200 C., 400 F., gas mark 6 for 2 hours, with greaseproof paper protecting the duck. Baste and remove the greaseproof towards end of cooking, allowing about 1/2 hour for the duck to brown. The remaining hot water can top up the juices in the tin. Bring to table garnished with parsley.

Apple Scone

8 oz wholemeal flour	2 teaspoons baking powder
1/4 teaspoon cinnamon	2 oz butter
2 oz brown sugar	8 oz cooking apples
milk to mix and glaze	

Preheat oven to 200 C., 400 F., gas mark 6. Sift flour, baking powder and spice into a bowl. Rub in the butter till the mixture resembles bread crumbs. Stir in sugar, peel core and grate the apples and mix into the flour etc. Add a very little milk to make a soft dough. Shape into a round on a floured board and brush with milk. Bake in oven for 25 minutes. Allow to cool, then split, buttering thickly.

The New Inn, Clovelly, well known for seafoods and cider in the 1920's when this photograph was taken, shows the fimiliar Clovelly sight of patient donkeys traversing the cobbled High Street. With their basket-work panniers, they have done so over a hundred years, usually attended by a fisherman.

Amber

ͻz short pastry	1 1/2 lb apples
+ oz demerara sugar	2 eggs
2 oz butter	1 oz caster sugar
1/2 cup water	

Peel core, cut the apples and stew them with the sugar and water until they fall. Mash them well with a wooden spoon and add the butter. Separate whites of eggs from yolks. Break up yolks and stir into the fruit mixture. Line the sides of the pie dish with a strip of pastry, crimping the edges. Pour in the fruit. Beat the whites of the eggs stiffly then mix in the ounce of caster sugar and pile it on top of the fruit. Bake in a hot oven for only 20 minutes.

Raspberry Tartlets

3/4 lb short pastry	1 lb raspberries
1 lb sugar	1/2 gill water
1 gill cream	

Place the washed fruit in a pan with the sugar and water. Stew gently for 5 minutes. Strain the fruit and put in a basin, returning the syrup to the pan. Boil it until it becomes a thick syrup reducing by half. Line 15 deep patty tins with shortcrust pastry and place a piece of greaseproof paper filled with rice in each. Bake for 15 minutes in a hot oven. Remove the rice and paper and when cool put a little of the fruit in each tartlet and pour a spoonful of syrup over it. Served with clotted cream heaped on each, these tartlets are delicious.

Strawberries and clotted cream is everbody's favourite and our June/July trips to Devon leave happy memories of the 'Strawberry boys' alongside large signs on the busy roads, their barrows stacked high in the early morning, but empty boxes piled by evening.

Custard Pudding from Chudleigh

2 eggs	1 pint milk
1 oz sugar	nutmeg
3 thin slices bread and butter	2 oz sultanas

Place the slices of bread and butter and the sultanas at the bottom of a buttered dish. Beat the eggs with the sugar and pour the milk onto them. Pour gently over the bread etc., distributing evenly, and grate a little nutmeg over the top. This delicious pudding should be cooked in a very moderate oven until set, which takes about 40 minutes.

A fine photograph of Tor Point and Ferry, Devonport, in the early years of the century. The old town contained all the naval establishments and dockyards. There is, however, an Old Town Hall, modelled on the Parthenon and other unusual buildings, the work of architect John Foulston who designed also for Plymouth.

Rough Cider from Okehampton

8 lb apples	8 lb sugar
4 lemons	1 fair-sized piece ginger root
2 gallons boiling water	

Place the washed apples in a wooden tub and crush them. Pour the boiling water over them, cover with a scalded cloth and leave for a fortnight. Daily mash up the apples. After the fortnight strain off liquor and put in the bruised ginger root and 1/2 lb sugar to every pint of cider. Add a little extra boiling water. Stir well and put in the lemon juice and the halved lemon cases. Leave for another 2 weeks. Skim off any scum. Remove the lemon halves and ginger root and bottle lightly for 3 days, after which the tops can be firmly fixed and the cider left for 2 months before drinking.

Another untested recipe, but we were warned of its potency. In the past, abuse of cider led to many a fight amongst labourers and seamen, but the number of apple recipes in this little book alone shows how fond the Devon people are of the cause of Adam and Eve's downfall.

On the Twelfth Night, cider was poured onto the roots of the apple trees and wassailing commenced.

"Here's to the old apple tree etc.
Hats full, caps full, bushel sacks full."

Blackberry and Apple Flummery

1 lb blackberries	1 lb apples
1/2 pint water	2 oz flour
1/2 teaspoon mixed spice	sugar to taste

Clean and pick the blackberries, peel and core the apples. Stew the fruit in water, sweeten to taste and press through a sieve. Mix the flour and spice to a smooth liquid with a little cold water. Boil the fruit puree and pour it on the flour, stirring well. Return the mixture to the pan and stir till it boils. Boil for 5 minutes and when cool enough, pour into a glass dish. When cold, serve with Devonshire cream. Raspberries, redcurrants or blackcurrants also make a good flummery.

Nuns' Cross, Dartmouth, photographed and initialled in June 1905, gives some idea of the vastness and wild quality of the Moor. Covering an area of 365 square miles, it is the most southerly National Park in Britain. Left from the neolithic period onwards, tombs, hut circles, standing stones, crosses, are found on Dartmoor, indicating past civilisations, but the story of the Nuns' cross I never discovered.

Nuns' Cross, Dartmoor

ner Pudding

In five regions I have found this pudding a great favourite, particularly in fruit-growing areas. The fruit can be varied: this one used blackcurrants.

1 1/2 lb blackcurrants	6 oz sugar
1/2 small, stale loaf	1/2 pint cream

Pick the fruit, wash and stew with a little water and sugar. Cut the bread into thick slices 1/3 inch and line a pudding basin with them. Pour in the hot fruit and place a thick slice of bread on top cut into a round shape. Stand the pudding in a wide soup plate and put a weight on top. Leave it for a day, then turn it out carefully and serve with thick cream.

At home, trying this out for the umpteenth time, I used damsons as it was coming to the end of year. We did not wonder why Summer Pudding was popular. The sharp, wine-like damsons with the cream were particularly good.

Chestnut Savoury

1 lb chestnuts	seasoning
1 egg	2 oz butter
1/4 teaspoon mixed dried herbs	1 oz flour
	1/4 teaspoon mustard
2 oz grated cheese	1 gill milk

Slit the chestnuts on the flat slide and put them in a tin a hot oven for 15 minutes. When the shells begin to split open, remove and peel off inner skins. Boil the chestnuts for 20 minutes and strain off water.

Mash them and place in a pan with 1 1/2 oz butter, mustard and herbs. Add the flour and mix well. Put in the milk and stir until it boils. Season and add nearly all the cheese and a well-beaten egg. Put into a fireproof dish and sprinkle with the rest of the cheese. Dot bits of butter on top and bake for 10 minutes in a hot oven. It is very good with watercress and sliced tomatoes.

Verderers in the south-west of England might also in some cases be petty constables. A verderer was an officer responsible for the King's forest. The post, held for life, dates back to the 11th century. There were four to each forest who attended the court of Attachment every 40 days and punished minor offences. There were also wood-reeves or forest-keepers. Horse-shoe shaped groups of stones with the open end facing a stream were called deer roasts and were used for cooking venison when it became permissible in some cases to shoot or cull deer.

Appropriate to Old Devon Recipes is a 1932 postcard issued by F.W. Broughton of the Old Inn, Widdecombe-in-the-Moors, and also its subject. 'Widecombe Green Tea Rooms'. The homely 'teas' sign is one of hundreds, less homely today, but the ancient, thatched, granite cottages clustered round the Green remain very attractive. The bowmen of Widdlecombe used to practise archery after church on the 'butte park' or village green.

Widecombe Green, Tea Rooms.

Haunch of Venison

After being hung, the venison should be allowed to marinate for three days, turning gently.

- the Marinade

1 pint vinegar	1/2 pint olive oil
3 pints red wine	1 clove of garlic
1 bayleaf	a few cloves
1 medium sized sliced onion	

The prepared haunch is spread with melted butter and well sprinkled with salt and pepper. Make a flour and water paste and roll it out after kneading it well. It must be big enough to cover the haunch of venison. Bake it in a moderate oven for 3 hours. The timing depends on size. After this peel off the hardened paste and return the joint to a hot oven to brown. The paste prevents undue drying out of the flesh which tends to dryness. My grandmother used to cook venison in a terracotta lidded pot, with trotters. The National Park at Exmoor has the largest wild herd of red deer outside Scotland.

Devonshire Pasty

6 oz cooked salmon	2 beaten eggs
3 tablespoons milk	seasoning
8 oz shortcrust pastry	

Make the pastry and let it rest in a cool pantry for an hour. Place the beaten eggs and milk in a basin. Make sure all bones are out of the fish and mix it in with the egg and milk. Add seasoning. Roll the pastry out and cut into rounds. Put filling into each round, pouring on a little of egg and milk mixed. Moisten edges of rounds and fit on a pastry top, crimping and sealing the pastry. Brush with more egg and bake in a moderate oven.

Shortcrust Pastry

1 lb flour	8 oz lard
6 tablespoons cold water	a little milk

Sift the flour then rub in the lard lightly with the fingers until the mixture resembles breadcrumbs. Add the water carefully so that the resultant pastry is not sticky. It should come cleanly away from the bowl and feel soft.

Devonshire pasties can also be filled with fruit, apple pasty seemingly being the most popular, but 1989 was a wonderful summer for apples. Markets at South Molton, Tiverton, Newton Abbot, Bideford, Barnstaple etc. were loaded with Cox's, Lord Lambourne, Russet, Bramley, Charles Ross.

Bream with Egg Sauce

Fresh fish is always stiff and firm and any colours are bright. A bream of 3 lb weight is suitable. Remove the scales, scraping from tail to head with a knife. Cut off the fins. Slit down the body and remove the inside. The black skin on the inside of the fish should be removed by rubbing with salt. Wash, and simmer for 15 minutes in water containing 2 tablespoons of tarragon vinegar.

the Egg Sauce

1 hard-boiled egg
1 1/2 oz flour
1 gill milk
1 dessertspoon chopped
parsley

1 1/2 oz butter
1/2 pint fish stock
salt and pepper

Melt the butter. Stir in the flour, milk and stock and boil, stirring all the time. Cut egg in half, chopping the white. Add it to the sauce. Season to taste. Boil for 3 minutes with the parsley and pour the sauce over the fish, which should meanwhile have been kept warm.

At Ottery St. Mary, as in other Devonshire towns, On November 5th flaming tar barrels were rolled down the street. In Victorian times these revels, connected with Guy Fawkes Night, often got out of hand, resulting in injury and much destruction to property. Hatherleigh did likewise on November 5th. just before daybreak and at nightfall when a torchlight procession was held. Almost certainly these rituals would originate in the Celtic fire-raising ceremony called Samain. Treacle Toffee, Devon butter or gingerbread eating seem a much better idea these days.

This magnificient door on the church St. Saviour, Dartmouth, is clearly dated 1631 but the iron figures of the beasts guarding the symbolic Tree of Life are thought to be even earlier. In many such ancient churches provision for a 'dole' of bread was often made in the wills of rich parishioners, the loaves to be given to the poor, needy and old who came to church.

...s toffee recipe is 80 years old and was simply called "TOFFY".

Take 3 lbs of the best brown sugar and boil with 1 1/2 pints of water until the candy hardens in coldwater. Then add 1/2 lb of sweet flavoured fresh butter which will soften the toffy. Boil a few minutes until it again hardens and pour it into trays. It may be flavoured with lemon."

An equally old recipe makes "plot treacle toffy" from 1 lb white sugar, 1 cup treacle, 1/2 cup water, 1 teaspoon cream of tartar, boiling slowly. After boiling for 20 minutes, try it by dropping some in cold water. If it "snaps" it is done. Pour into buttered tin dishes.

Devon Cream Toffee

Melt 1 lb crushed sugar into 1/4 lb butter. When nearly melted add by degrees 1/2 pint cream, stirring all the time. Boil until it is so thick you can hardly turn the spoon. Turn it into a tin which has been buttered. Smooth it with a clean knife. In a few minutes it will be ready to cut into squares. Quarter of an hour is usually long enough to boil it, but be careful for it easily burns. Stir without ceasing. Add 1/4 teaspoon vanilla just before finished.

Bideford Tripe Soup

1/2 lb tripe	1 rasher fatty bacon
1 parsnip	1 pint water
1 pint milk	1 dessertspoon wholemeal
seasoning	flour
1 lb Spanish onions	

Wash the tripe well and cut into small pieces. Peel and chop the onions finely. The parsnip should be washed, scraped and chopped. Cut the bacon small also. With the seasoning put all these into a big stew pan with the milk and water. Bring to boiling point and skim, then simmer slowly for 1 1/2 hours. Mix the flour and water to a thin paste and add to the soup, which should never at any point in the long simmering boil fast. Stir for 5 minutes until the soup thickens, then it can be served. A hundred years ago this was reckoned a cheap, strengthening soup for people recovering from illness.

Edward Capern was the postman poet of Bideford. After his death in 1894 the bell which he carried on his rounds was placed in a niche on his tombstone at Heanton Punchardon.

Devonshire Junket

To one quart of warm milk add one tablespoon of brandy and one tablespoon of sugar. Pour into a china dish with two teaspoons of rennet. When set, spread thick Devonshire cream over the top. Grate a little nutmeg over the cream and from the sugar caster, sprinkle a little sparkling sugar.

Damson Jam

4 lb damsons
4 lb sugar
1/2 pint water

Simmer the washed, ripe damsons in the water until soft. Skim off stones as they surface. Stir in the sugar. Bring to boil and keep stirring until a set is reached. Pot straight away.

Horrabridge village is between Tavistock and Plymouth, this scene dating from the early years of 1900 when the chief source of employment was provided by the Horrabridge Brick Works. The bridge where the three girls and small boy are standing has its brick wall made from local clay. Jugged hare or rabbit with cream could have been part of the day's fare for these charming-looking children.

Widdecombe Fairings

2 oz flour	2 oz unsalted butter
1 dessertspoon caster sugar	2 oz syrup
1/2 oz ground ginger (optional)	

Warm the butter in a pan, then take off the fire and stir in flour, syrup and sugar. A flat toffee tin should be buttered and into this mixture placed in small spoonfuls, leaving room to spread. Bake in a hot oven for 10 minutes. Remove from tin with a palette knife and curve them round the handle of a wooden spoon. If they are to be filled with Devonshire clotted cream they need to be curled tightly.

The famous fair at Widdecombe may well be the oldest in England. Spiced ale was traditional besides fairings, a word which applied to a host of novelties, not merely the sweetmeat on the gingerbread stall. There were trays of neck and shoulder ribbons, tin lockets with glass stones. Over a century ago the merry-go-round was trundled full circle by two heavy horses. There was the panorama showing some historical event, the coconut shy, the fighting booth and the shooting gallery. At the general fairs Devonshire merchants "offered serges, shalloons and kerseys".

Spiced Ale

4 pints ale	2 teaspoons sugar
2 sliced Cox's apples	pinch of spice
pinch of nutmeg	3 whole cloves

Heat slowly but do not allow to boil. Add all ingredients except apple. Take off the heat and keep warm by the fire for 15 minutes. Strain and put in the apple slices in a punch bowl with ladle.

Barnstaple Fair dates from the Middle Ages. Its opening takes place at the Guildhall, when spiced ale, brewed from a closely guarded Elizabethan recipe, is ladled into silver cups. All present drink success to the fair. Above their heads hangs a large, white glove, the ancient symbol which used to show outsiders that they could enter the fair and trade freely in the town.

Frumenty

Sold at the fairs, was made from crushed whole wheat, sugar, allspice, raisins and skimmed milk, simmered in an earthenware pot in the fire oven overnight. Another popular fairing.

Rose Water

Gather one pint of fragrant, scented rose petals on a still, dry day. Place in a basin and cover with one pint of boiling water that has been filtered first. Leave to infuse for at least an hour. Strain through a sieve and pour into bottles. Cork lightly and use as tonic to splash on face or body.

Pot Pourri

Gather and dry a quantity of fragrantly scented rose petals. Mix one dessertspoon of powdered borax with the same of salt and one teaspoon of powdered cinnamon. The mixture should then be added to two quarts of dried rose petals and stirred well. The fragrance of pot pourri is released when the bowls are left in warm sunshine, in porches or on window ledges facing south.

Above the River Salcombe estuary lies Kingsbridge, which had an active coastal trade in the 19th.
century, with shipbuilding yard and cattle market. This 1905 postcard shows the Market Arcade,
restored in 1796. Lavish hospitality at Kingsbridge was noted for centuries, especially the brewing
of 'white ale' served at the King's Arms. It was made from an old German recipe and said to
be 'made on Saturday and tapped on Sunday'.

Acknowledgements

I should like to thank:

Barnstaple Library
Barnstaple Record Office
Glenys Battams
Bideford Library
Shirley Booker
Evelyn Boyd
Stanley Butterworth
Clovelly Village Centre
Dartmoor National
Park Devon County Library
Captain Enthovens
Exmoor National Park-Information Centre,
North Devon
The Exmoor Visitor
Joyce Gooding
Michael and Anne Gornall
Eric Hayes

Mary Hobbs
Nicola Johns
Angela Lewin
Loddiswell Vineyard
Michelle Luke
Patricia Macarthy
Adam McElroy
Eve Martin
Mid-Devon Tourist Association
The National Trust
North Devon Farm Park
North Devon Museum
Carol Nott
Margaret Paice
Janet and Richard Pelling
Valerie Rooke
E.G.Rothwell

Sonnenheim Hotel, Bideford
Jack Stasiak
David Taylor
Mr. S.R.A.Taylor
Tors Hotel, Lynmouth
Tourist Information Centres:
Barnstaple
Bideford
Ilfracombe
Lynmouth
South Molton
Torquay
Tom Tulley
Mrs.Webster
Wool Marketing Board, S. Moltor

To all others whose names went unrecorded-our sincere thanks for being so kind and co-operative.